Merry Christmas, Tess!
From Mrs. Lange 2010

CONCORDIA PUBLISHING HOUSE · SAINT LOUIS

GOD'S LOVE AT
Christmas

Stephanie Jeffs and John Haysom

A long time ago, in a town called Nazareth,
something very special happened....

It had all happened so quickly.
Mary had been sweeping the floor.
It was something she did every
morning, before the day grew too hot.

Suddenly the room filled with the whitest of lights. It was unlike any other light she had ever seen.

"Mary," a voice said. The sound of her name made her look up into the light. It was beautiful. She knew at once that this was an angel sent from God.

"Do not be afraid," said the angel. "God is with you. You have no reason to be afraid. I am Gabriel. I have come to tell you that God is pleased with you. You will become pregnant and have a baby boy—God's own Son. He will be the Savior of the world."

The words were incredible, but Mary believed them.

And now, here she was, leaving the town of Nazareth with, Joseph, who was to be her husband. Mary was expecting a baby that she knew was God's own Son.

A census had been ordered by the Roman emperor, who wanted to know how many people lived in his land so he could tax them. Joseph and Mary were going to Bethlehem with many other people because it was the town Joseph's family had come from: the City of David.

Joseph guided the donkey and helped Mary as they travelled together.

When they finally saw the ancient town of Bethlehem ahead of them, Mary felt relieved. But Joseph could tell from a distance that the town was unusually crowded. There were people everywhere, people who had come to the town to be counted for the emperor's census.

There was only one inn in Bethlehem. The noise from the open windows indicated how full it was. So Joseph was not surprised by the innkeeper's response.

Have I got a room?"
said the innkeeper.
He looked hot and tired,
and beads of sweat
sparkled on his forehead.
"I haven't got a space
anywhere. Try one of the
houses." He shut
the door.

Joseph tried the
houses. They were all
full. It was hopeless.
Before long he found
himself back at the inn.
He stopped outside the door
and knocked again.

"Sir," he said, "I know
that you do not have any
room in your inn, but my
wife is pregnant and will
soon give birth.

"I have tried everywhere," Joseph explained, "but there is no room. Do you know of anywhere where we can rest tonight?"

The innkeeper wiped his forehead with the back of his hand. He looked at Mary and then at Joseph.

"I can think of only one place," he said. He pointed to a building beside the inn —the stable. "Stay there, if you want."

"Thank you," said Joseph. He turned round and pulled the donkey toward the stable.

It was dark in the stable (and smelly), but it was quiet and calm away from the crowds. Mary tried to rest.

She felt her body tighten and knew that very soon she would give birth to her special baby.

Joseph tethered the donkey at one end of the stable. He kicked away the dirty, soiled straw and scattered what was clean over the hard ground.

There, in the stable, Mary gave birth to her first child, a son. She took Him in her arms and held Him, while He took His first breaths of air. She smiled as He nuzzled against her, and she stroked the soft, dark hair on His head. She placed her little finger in the palm of His tiny hand and felt His gentle grip.

Joseph knelt beside her and watched them both. Then he took the newborn baby in his arms and carefully placed his hand on the baby's head.

"Welcome, Jesus!" he said.

Mary tore some cloth into long strips, which she wrapped around Jesus. Then she picked Him up and gently laid Him in the manger.

It was cold on the hills outside Bethlehem.

A group of shepherds stood in the entrance of the sheep fold. The fire had almost died down, and all that remained were deep red, glowing embers.

Suddenly, a dazzling light filled the night sky. A voice spoke from deep within the light and echoed round the hillside. "Do not be afraid!" said the voice.

Instantly, a peacefulness came over the shepherds. They stopped trembling and slowly stood up. Within the light they saw the outline of an angel.

"I have good news for you and for the whole world!" said the angel.

"A baby has been born tonight in Bethlehem. He is God's Son, and He will save the world. You can go and see Him for yourselves. You will find Him wrapped in strips of cloth, lying in a manger."

Then the shepherds saw hundreds of other angels. They danced across the sky, and as they danced, they sang: "Glory to God in the highest heaven. Peace to His people on earth!"

The sound of the singing made the earth tremble, and the shepherds moved with the music of the song. They sang with the angels. "Glory to God!" they sang, "Peace on earth!"

Gradually the singing grew quieter and the light became more dim, until the darkness of the night returned. The shepherds were alone on the hillside.

They stood still, until one of them finally spoke. "Did the angel really say that God's Son was born tonight?" he asked, voicing the thoughts of them all.

"Yes," said another. "I heard it too."

"Let's go!" said one of the shepherds, picking up his staff. He turned to his friends and began to laugh. "What are we waiting for? Let's go to find this baby in Bethlehem!"

The shepherds ran down to Bethlehem and through the streets until they found the stable.

They paused in the entrance and saw Mary and Joseph. Then they went in. It was as if Mary and Joseph were expecting them.

They gathered around the manger and saw the tiny newborn baby, swaddled tightly  in strips of cloth, lying on the hay. The shepherds sank to their knees.

"Glory to God!" they whispered.
"This *is* the Savior of the world!"
"His name is Jesus," Joseph
told them.

15

As the baby Jesus slept, the shepherds told Mary and Joseph everything that had happened that night. They talked about the angels and the song that they had sung. They talked about the birth of Jesus, God's own Son, and they praised God together for all that had happened.

As dawn broke, and the shepherds left the stable to spread the news of the Savior's birth to everyone they saw,
At last, Mary closed her eyes. *Nothing is impossible with God!* she thought, and she lay back, waiting to hear the morning cries of her newborn baby, Jesus.

Many miles away, in another country, some Wise Men were studying the stars. They searched through ancient charts and documents until they were certain that what they had seen in the sky was true. A bright new star shone in the night sky. It had appeared suddenly and without warning. It was bigger and brighter than any other star in the universe.

"It is the star for a new King," said one wise man to the others, and he pointed to his chart. "There is no doubt. This star shows that an important new king has just been born!"

The Wise Men looked at one another excitedly.

As quickly as they could, they packed for their journey. They did not know how long it would take them or where they were going.

But they were sure that if they followed the star, they would find the new King. And because they were certain of what they would find, they brought with them presents of gold, frankincense and myrrh.

Eight days after Jesus was born, Mary and Joseph took Him to be circumcised, according to Jewish law.

"What will you call the child?" Joseph was asked.

"His name is Jesus," he replied.

Six weeks later, they loaded their donkey to travel to Jerusalem to present Jesus in the temple. Joseph carried two young doves, which he would offer as a sacrifice to God.

At the temple, an old man stared intently at Mary and the baby she was holding. He slowly made his way toward her, picking his way through the crowd.

20

Mary handed Jesus to the old man.

The man, whose name was Simeon, cradled the child in his arms, and then he spoke, his eyes overflowing with tears. "Holy Lord," he said. "You have kept Your promise to me. I have seen the Savior of the world!"

Simeon handed Jesus back to Mary. Mary and Joseph looked at each other. They were too amazed to speak.

At that moment, an old woman called Anna came up to them. She smiled and her face lit up with joy as she praised God. And like the shepherds, Anna told everyone she saw that the Savior had come.

Mary and Joseph made their way back to Bethlehem, thinking of all the things they had heard and seen in Jerusalem. They were unaware of the other travellers who had begun their journey to visit them.

The palace in Jerusalem stood high above the city. The Wise Men made their way through the cobbled streets, riding on camels. They did not stop anywhere else, but went straight to the palace.

The king, Herod, was surprised that he had foreign visitors. He was not expecting them. He was even more surprised when he heard why they had come.

"Sire," they said, as they bowed before him. "We have come to see the new king, who has been born the King of the Jews. We saw His star rise in the East, and we have come to worship Him."

Herod frowned. "How interesting," he said. He left the Wise Men and called his advisers.

"Tell me," Herod said to his advisors, "does it say anything in our ancient

writings about where God's
Savior King will be born?"

"In Bethlehem," the advisors replied.

But I am the only king! thought Herod.

He returned to the Wise Men. "Our ancient
Scriptures say the king you are looking for will be
found in Bethlehem. Go there, and look for the child.
Then, when you have found Him, come and tell me where
He lives. I, too, would like to worship Him."

But Herod lied. He wanted to destroy the new King.

The Wise Men left the palace and made their way to
Bethlehem.

"Look!" said one of the men, as they stepped outside
the palace, into the night. "The star!"

There in the sky was the star they had seen months before.
It hung in the sky as a sign, showing the way to Bethlehem,
to where Mary and Joseph and Jesus lived.

As soon as the Wise Men arrived in Bethlehem and saw the house, they knew they were at the right place. They knocked on the door, and Mary opened it.

She was not expecting visitors, and had never seen men like them before. But she was not surprised that they had come.

24

"You have come to see the Child?" she asked.

They nodded, and she ushered them in.

Mary took the Child into her arms.

One by one the Wise Men knelt before Him. Then they unwrapped the presents they had brought with them.

The child Jesus smiled and clapped His hands when He saw them.

The gold sparkled even in the dull light, and the smell of the myrrh and the frankincense filled the house.

Then the Wise Men left, overjoyed that they had seen the baby King.

It was late, and the men had yet to return to Jerusalem to see King Herod as they had promised. They stopped for the night and fell asleep, thinking of everything they had seen in the tiny house. When they woke the next morning, they were all uneasy.

"I had a strange dream," said one of the men as they prepared to leave.

"So did I!" said another. "I do not think we should return to Jerusalem."

"Neither do I," agreed a third. "Let's go home another way."

That night, Joseph, too, lay thinking about the men who had come to see Jesus.

He fell into a restless sleep. Suddenly, he sat upright. It was still dark.

Gently, he woke Mary. "Mary," he whispered. "Get up!"

Mary rubbed her eyes.

"I've had a dream," said Joseph urgently. "An angel came to me with a message. King Herod wants to kill Jesus. We must run away, to Egypt!"

Quickly, Mary and Joseph gathered up as many things as they could and loaded them on to their donkey. They fled to Egypt in the dark of night. Together, Joseph, Mary, and Jesus escaped Herod's wickedness.

And they lived in Egypt until the day came that they could safely return to Nazareth.

This edition published 2010 by Concordia Publishing House
3558 South Jefferson Avenue • St. Louis, MO 63118-3968
www.cph.org • 1-800-325-3040
ISBN 978-0-7586-2543-4

This story is a retelling of the accounts made by the Gospel writers,
and is based on Matthew 1:18—2:15 and Luke 1:1—38; 2:1—38.

Editorial Director Annette Reynolds
Art Director Gerald Rogers

Pre-production Manager Krystyna Kowalska Hewitt
Production Manager John Laister

Printed and bound in Singapore
Singapore / 000920 / 300329